Roll out the red rug.

3

Here comes the new king!

4

Roll Out the
Red Rug

Written by David Bauer
Illustrated by Lane Yerkes

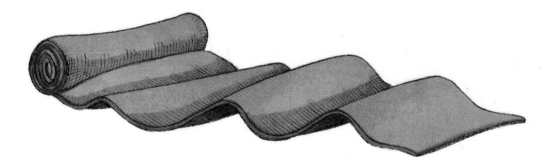

Modern Curriculum Press
A Division of Simon & Schuster
299 Jefferson Road, P.O. Box 480
Parsippany, NJ 07054 - 0480

Design and production by MKR Design, Inc.

ISBN: 0-8136-2060-0 Modern Curriculum Press

1 2 3 4 5 6 7 8 9 10 SP 01 00 99 98 97 96 95

Tap on the drum.

Here comes the new king!

Grab the flag.

Here comes the new king!

9

Don't trip.

10

We don't want the rug to rip.

Quick!

Get the rug.

Get the drum.

Get the flag.

Get ready.

13

Here comes the new king!

"Stop!

I'm not the king!"

Roll out the red rug.

Here comes the new king!